~~~~~~~~~~~~~~~

Gift of the
Hackbarth Foundation
2015

~~~~~~~~~~~~~~~

THE
JAPANESE
INTERNMENT
CAMPS

A HISTORY PERSPECTIVES BOOK

Rachel A. Bailey

Published in the United States of America by Cherry Lake Publishing
Ann Arbor, Michigan
www.cherrylakepublishing.com

Consultants: Greg Robinson, PhD, Professor of American History,
Université du Québec À Montréal; Marla Conn, ReadAbility, Inc.
Editorial direction: Red Line Editorial
Book design and illustration: Sleeping Bear Press

Photo Credits: Ansel Adams/Library of Congress, cover (left), cover
(middle), cover (right), 1 (left), 1 (middle), 1 (right), 4, 14, 19, 26, 28;
Bettmann/Corbis, 6, 22; AP Images, 10; Library of Congress, 12; U.S. Army
Signal Corps/AP Images, 21; U.S. Army Signal Corps/Library of Congress, 30

Library of Congress Cataloging-in-Publication Data

Bailey, Rachel A.
 The Japanese internment camps / Rachel A. Bailey.
    pages cm. -- (Perspectives library)
 Includes index.
 ISBN 978-1-62431-666-1 (hardcover) -- ISBN 978-1-62431-693-7 (pbk.)
-- ISBN 978-1-62431-720-0 (pdf) -- ISBN 978-1-62431-747-7 (hosted
ebook)
 1. Japanese Americans--Evacuation and relocation, 1942-1945--Juvenile
literature. 2. World War, 1939-1945--Japanese Americans--Juvenile
literature. 3. Japanese--United States--History--Juvenile literature. I. Title.

 D769.8.A6B325 2013
 940.53'17089956073--dc23
                       2013029718

Cherry Lake Publishing would like to acknowledge the work of
The Partnership for 21st Century Skills. Please visit www.p21.org
for more information.

Printed in the United States of America
Corporate Graphics Inc.
January 2014

TABLE OF CONTENTS

In this book, you will read about the Manzanar War Relocation Center, a Japanese internment camp, from three perspectives. Each perspective is based on real things that happened to real people who lived in Manzanar in the 1940s. As you'll see, the same event can look different depending on one's point of view.

Helen Watanabe
Child at the Manzanar War Relocation Center

I will never forget December 7, 1941, the day that turned my world upside down. My parents, my younger brother, Jack, and I had just gotten back from church in Los Angeles, California. Father switched on the radio. Within minutes, he barked at us all to be quiet. We listened as the radio announcer said that Japan had attacked Pearl Harbor in Hawaii just hours before.

On Monday, December 8, Mother kept us home from school. We are Japanese Americans, and she feared people might treat us and other Japanese Americans poorly because of the Pearl Harbor attack. It turned out she was right. The restaurant a block from our house posted a sign that said, "No Japs wanted!" Also, someone slashed the front tires of Father's car.

Many people suspected Japanese Americans were working for Japan, our enemy in the war. I have a

PEARL HARBOR

Just before 8:00 a.m. on December 7, 1941, Japanese pilots bombed Pearl Harbor, a military base in Hawaii, in a surprise attack. More than 3,500 people were killed or injured in the attack. The next day, the United States declared war on Japan and entered World War II.

◄ Japanese Americans faced prejudice and discrimination after the attack on Pearl Harbor.

hard time understanding why people didn't trust us. My parents were born in Japan, yes, but they have lived in the United States for 20 years. They are loyal to this country.

The people who thought we were dangerous wanted our removal from the West Coast. Their political representatives brought the requests to Washington. I think this helped influence President Franklin Roosevelt to sign Executive Order 9066 in February 1942. The order allowed the United States to remove people from military areas "as deemed necessary or desirable." Military areas were soon defined as the entire West Coast. Father said the government thought Japanese Americans were plotting with Japan to attack the West

Coast. Roosevelt's order would allow the U.S. Army to remove Japanese Americans from this area.

Over the next few weeks, Mother frantically tried to sell as many of our possessions as possible. She thought we would be forced from our homes very soon. People bought our books, toys, linens, and even our dog for next to nothing. I'll never forget the tear that trickled down Jack's face as Father carried Max, our beloved mutt, out the door. That was the last time we would ever see him. When I tried to console Jack, Father whispered, "Shikata ga nai." It means, "It cannot be helped."

In early May 1942, our family received notice we were going to have to vacate our home. In the middle of the month, my family left our home and boarded a bus to the Owens Valley Reception Center, later named the Manzanar War Relocation Center. We held duffel bags stuffed with our belongings. We could take only what we could carry. At the bus station, the

U.S. military police gave us tags with numbers on them. These numbers were our new identity. For the next three and a half years, our family was known as 35456. We followed our orders and secured the tags onto our coat collars.

Arriving at the center, I couldn't believe we were still in California. The vast desert wasteland was so different from our coastal community that had trees and shrubs. The landscape and the barbed wire surrounding the facility made it look like a prison. It was an **internment** center, but I felt it was a type of prison. Armed guards met us at our new home. They fingerprinted us and searched our bodies for kitchen knives and knitting needles. We were not allowed to have these items.

After inspection, the center's staff explained that Manzanar was like a miniature city. It sat on 6,200 acres of land. It had a school, a baseball field, and a hospital. It also had blocks of housing. Each of the

36 blocks contained 14 **barracks**. Each barracks housed four one-room apartments. Our address was block 10, barracks 9, apartment 3.

A lone lightbulb hung from the ceiling of our apartment. An oil stove heated the room. Eight army cots with mattresses stuffed with straw and blankets completed the apartment. Another family of four joined us during our stay. Our apartment was quite cramped since it was about the size of our old living room. There was no bathroom in our apartment. The bathrooms were located in a separate barracks. If I had to go to the bathroom in the middle of the night, I had to wake Mother so she could walk there with me.

For dinner, our family went to the mess hall. We ate all our meals there since we didn't have a

SECOND SOURCE

▶ Find another source that describes the Japanese internment camps. Compare the information there to the information in this source.

kitchen. We stood in a long line for our food each night. The servers plopped canned wieners and beans onto our dirty plates. At first, we were not given any vegetables or rice, which are staple foods for my family and many other Japanese Americans.

In the fall, Jack and I attended school at Manzanar. Jack started first grade, and I began fourth. I must say I actually liked school. Manzanar was a safe place for

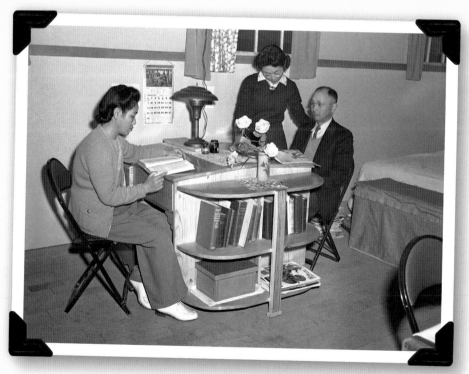

▲ *Families lived in one-room apartments.*

us. After the Pearl Harbor attack, we often got hateful stares and comments from students and even teachers at our old school. Those were all gone now. Except for the center's workers, everyone here was a Japanese American.

Manzanar soon began to feel like a tight-knit community. I made friends, and we had opportunities to get involved. Jack joined the baseball team, and I participated in the glee club and took up baton twirling. Father supported our family as a farm worker in the area fields for $16 per month. Mother worked as a waitress in the mess hall for $12 per month. Sometimes it seemed like we weren't even in the camp.

Things were calm until one late December afternoon in 1942. Jack and I played marbles while

THINK ABOUT IT

▶ Determine the main point of this paragraph. Pick out one piece of evidence to support your answer.

Mother hemmed Father's pants. We heard a lot of yelling outside our barracks. Then we heard several gunshots. Mother cautiously cracked the door. We peered through the crack and saw an angry mob surrounded by military police. Later, we learned the police killed two **internees** and injured ten. That was the scariest thing I experienced at Manzanar. I was frightened that might happen to my parents.

A week later, I overheard Father telling Mother that the Manzanar **Riot** occurred when six male internees beat up Fred Tayama, one of the leaders of the Japanese

Many internees worked in the fields. ▶

American Citizens League (JACL). The JACL is a group that works to protect the rights of Japanese Americans. Tension had arisen between some internees and the JACL because of disagreements about how the group worked to get rights for Japanese Americans. The next day, three men were put in jail for beating the JACL leader. Many people felt that the men were unfairly accused. A crowd of more than 1,000 people gathered to protest their arrest in front of the camp administration. Military police were not able to keep order in such a large crowd, and a riot ensued.

We left Manzanar in 1945, right before it closed. This was difficult for us since Mother and Father didn't have jobs outside the camp. Luckily, some members of our former church found us a place to stay until my parents found work. Living at Manzanar was both a curse and a blessing. I hated how the government imprisoned us to ease their suspicions, but loved the sense of community I found there.

Mas Yubu

Japanese-American Soldier

I was a freshman at the University of California, Los Angeles when a classmate told me Japan had attacked Pearl Harbor early on December 7, 1941. I was saddened so many people had died. But I didn't think the news would impact me personally. Boy, was I wrong.

The next morning, I heard a loud knock on my dorm room door. When I opened the door, my mother and younger brother Hy were waiting for me. My mother told me my father was gone. Between sobs, she explained to me how the Federal Bureau of Investigation (FBI) had taken Father from our home late last night. She thought they distrusted him because he was a leader in our community. After the Pearl Harbor attack, the FBI unfairly jailed many Japanese Americans who were community leaders and Japanese language teachers. They thought these people with Japanese **ancestry** were a threat to national security. Because of Father's departure, I left school and moved back into my childhood home.

Life was difficult without him. He was our rock and the main provider for the family. He moved to the United States in 1915 when he was only 19. He was from the first generation of Japanese to

ANALYZE THIS

► Compare the perspectives of Helen Watanabe and Mas Yubu. How are they similar? How are they different?

immigrate to the United States. Issei was the formal name given to his generation. Mother was also an Issei. Because of strict immigration laws, Father and Mother were not granted U.S. citizenship. Hy and I were Nisei, or second-generation Japanese Americans. Because we were born in California, we were both U.S. citizens.

In mid-March 1942, Hy and I noticed a sign posted on a telephone pole by our house. It required the evacuation of anyone of Japanese ancestry. During the following weeks, we gave away or sold as much as we could. We each packed a suitcase with as many of our belongings as we could carry. Mother, Hy, and I also divided up Father's personal items in our suitcases in hopes that he would rejoin us soon.

In April, we boarded a bus headed for the Owens Valley Reception Center, which was renamed the Manzanar War Relocation Center in June. Searchlights scanned the complex. Armed guards stood at attention, waiting for our arrival. Upon exiting the bus, we heard

JAPANESE INTERNMENT CAMPS

In 1942, the U.S. Army removed more than 120,000 Japanese Americans from their West Coast homes. They were held in ten different camps located mostly in deserts and swamplands in the western and central United States. Most camps had schools, hospitals, newspapers, and even baseball leagues and movie theaters. The War Relocation Authority (WRA) was the department that oversaw the large-scale internment of Japanese Americans.

a familiar voice shouting, "Yubu," our last name. Out of the corner of my eye, I saw Father running toward us. He hugged us tightly.

After our surprise reunion, Father told us that the FBI had accused him and many other Issei of being a threat to national defense. After four months in prison, he was allowed to plead his case. The FBI realized their error and released Father. Some Issei, unfortunately, were not reunited with their families until the end of World War II in 1945.

Father suggested I volunteer for the military. We both agreed this would be a way to prove my loyalty to the United States. Also, it would give me the freedom that I didn't have at Manzanar. When I made my request to a worker at the center, he told me all Japanese-American men were classified as "enemy aliens." They were not allowed to serve in the military. Only those who were already serving were allowed to stay.

I quickly learned that if we followed the rules and kept busy, life at Manzanar was bearable. I worked as an orderly at the hospital for $16 per month. In my free time, I participated in a baseball league, played cards, and even went to a couple dances.

Although I kept busy, I disliked very much that I was forced to stay at Manzanar. All that changed on February 6, 1943, when some people from the army visited camp. They gave all adults 17 or older in the camp a questionnaire. This determined how loyal we were to our country. It also determined whether we were willing to serve in the military. This was surprising, since a year ago we were not welcomed in the military. I passed the test, and was allowed to leave the camp and serve in the armed forces.

March was bittersweet. Tears welled up in my eyes as I said good-bye to my family. I was on my way to Camp Shelby, Mississippi, for basic training. This was

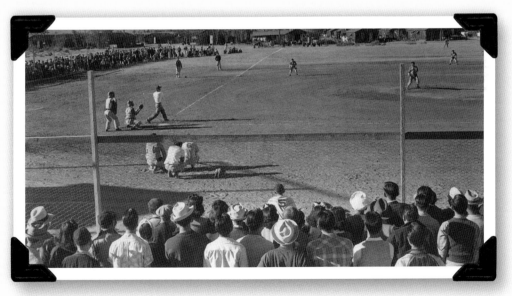

▲ *People played and watched baseball at the Manzanar War Relocation Center.*

my ticket out of Manzanar, but I felt so sad that I had to leave my family behind.

More than 3,000 of us trained at Camp Shelby. Our Japanese-American unit was called the 442nd Regimental Combat Team. Many of us Nisei wanted to prove our loyalty to the United States or die trying.

After ten months of training, the 442nd traveled overseas. We fought many battles in Italy and **liberated** several towns in France from **Nazi** rule. After only two days of rest, we were called to rescue a Texas **battalion** in October 1944. The members of the battalion were stuck in France surrounded by the Nazi army. They had no food or water. Our 442nd stepped in and rescued 215 of the members. Sadly, this cost the 442nd 400 of our own men.

In May 1945, the war ended in Europe. With no place to go,

SECOND SOURCE

▶ Find another source on the 442nd Regimental Combat Team and compare the information there to the information in this source.

I traveled back to Manzanar to stay with my family. I was very upset by this. I had risked my life for my country, and now I was back behind bars with my family. We left Manzanar in October 1945, about a month before the camp closed.

In 1946, President Harry Truman invited the members of the 442nd to a special ceremony in our honor. At the ceremony, he commended us for fighting the enemy. Then he told us to keep fighting prejudice and we would continue to win. This was just what I needed. I had proved I was a loyal American.

Members of the 442nd Regimental Combat Team remembered their fallen comrades during the war. ▶

Grace Jones
*Teacher at the Manzanar
War Relocation Center*

On Sunday, December 7, 1941, a friend and I were eating a late breakfast at a local café when we overheard that Japan had attacked Pearl Harbor just hours before. I rushed to my dorm room and switched on the radio.

I was hoping it was only a rumor. Unfortunately, the announcer confirmed it was true. In the weeks after the attacks, negative reports about Japanese Americans abounded. The headlines mentioned there could be Japanese submarines off the California coast. Japanese spies might be watching our every move. People started thinking all Japanese Americans were in on it. This **mass hysteria** got me to thinking about Nancy, a Japanese-American friend I met at college. She was one of the nicest people I knew. I couldn't believe people might think she was working against the United States.

THINK ABOUT IT

▶ Determine the main point of this paragraph. Pick out one piece of evidence that supports your answer.

Putting these thoughts aside, I focused on other pressing matters. I graduated from college in late December 1941, but my job prospects were not good. I blamed that on the war. This caused me to move back in with my parents.

In March, I read in the paper that the government mandated all Japanese Americans to vacate their West

Coast homes. Around that same time, my friend Nancy said she and her family would be leaving soon. The authorities required her family to live in a camp until further notice. A couple of weeks later, I stopped by Nancy's house to see how she was doing, but her family had already left.

By June, I was still reading the want ads when I noticed an ad from the WRA. The ad stated that several teachers were needed at one of ten Japanese relocation centers. I wasn't too excited about the opportunity. I applied for the job anyway since I didn't have other leads. I quickly got an interview. Two weeks later, I accepted a fourth-grade teaching job at the Manzanar War Relocation Center for $2,000 a year. Later, I found out that Japanese-American teachers made only $16 a month and $192 a year.

In September, my parents drove me to Manzanar. We piled as many of my belongings as we could in their car. Strong winds blew sand in our faces as we

TEACHERS

Not many internees had formal teacher training. Yet many of them were allowed to teach, even if they hadn't graduated from college. It was difficult to recruit trained teachers from outside the camps because living conditions were so poor in the camps.

stepped out of the car. My parents exchanged worried glances as they helped me get settled into my new desert home.

At first, I shared an apartment in block 7 with a female internee named Kim and her four-year-old daughter. A curtain divided our living quarters from my temporary classroom.

I had two days to prepare for school with minimal supplies. The room included a desk and a chair. The students had to sit on the floor. I had teacher textbooks for math, science, social studies, and reading. Students, however, did not have their own textbooks.

▲ *At Manzanar, students walked from their barracks to their classrooms.*

On the first day of school, 30 fourth graders stared at me with wide eyes while I introduced myself. Next, it was time to say the Pledge of Allegiance. All Manzanar students were required to recite this every day. The last line of the pledge, "with liberty and justice for all," upset me. These children were not experiencing our country's liberty and justice. Their families were forced to live behind barbed wire for doing nothing wrong.

Eventually, an entire block was dedicated to elementary students. There were 15 barracks in this block. The students in my classroom now had their own desks and chairs. Groups from various states donated textbooks and other school supplies. Although this allowed the children to study at home, I tried not to assign too much homework. Because of their tight living quarters, the children had a difficult time finding a quiet place for their studies. Even so, I encouraged them to document their time at Manzanar. Many kept diaries and sketched pictures about their experiences. They also wrote haiku, a Japanese form of poetry.

In 1943, I moved out of my apartment in block 7. The staff block was finally ready. I shared a dormitory room that included a bathroom with another teacher.

▲ *Japanese-American students in internment camps had few school supplies.*

Although this new staff block had its own mess hall and recreation club, we still ventured back to block 7 to socialize with Kim and the other Japanese Americans we had befriended.

I left Manzanar in the summer of 1945. Numerous families were finally allowed to leave camp, so not as many teachers were needed. Looking back, I'm glad my first teaching job was at Manzanar. I learned how fear can cause a government to discriminate against an entire race. I also met some of the most friendly, polite, and lovely people I've ever known.

ANALYZE THIS

▶ Compare this perspective with that of Mas Yubu, the Japanese-American soldier. How are they alike? How are they different?

LOOK, LOOK AGAIN

This photo shows Japanese Americans gathered at an assembly center. They went to an assembly center before being sent to an internment camp. Answer the following questions:

1. What would a Japanese-American child who had just been forced to leave his or her home think of this scene?

2. How would a Japanese-American soldier describe this scene to members of his battalion?

3. What would a schoolteacher who was not Japanese American think and notice about this scene?

GLOSSARY

ancestry (AN-ses-tree) the line of family a person comes from

barracks (BAR-uhks) groups of large, plain buildings that people live in

battalion (buh-TAL-yuhn) a large group of soldiers

immigrate (IM-i-grayt) to move to a new country that one is not originally from

internees (in-turn-EES) people who are in an internment camp

internment (in-TURN-muhnt) relating to forced confinement, often during war

liberated (LIB-uh-ray-ted) set free

mass hysteria (MAS hi-STER-ee-uh) unrealistic fear or reaction of a group of people that occurs after a major event

Nazi (NAHT-see) relating to the National Socialist German Workers' Party, which ruled Germany from 1933 to 1945

riot (RYE-uht) a loud, often violent public outburst by a large group of people

LEARN MORE

Further Reading

Cooper, Michael L. *Remembering Manzanar: Life in a Japanese Relocation Camp.* New York: Clarion Books, 2002.

Houston, Jeanne Wakatsuki, and James D. Houston. *Farewell to Manzanar: A True Story of Japanese American Experience during and after the World War II Internment.* New York: Ember, 2012.

Sakurai, Gail. *Japanese American Internment Camps.* New York: Children's Press, 2002.

Web Sites

Manzanar National Historic Site
http://www.nps.gov/history/museum/exhibits/manz/index.html
This Web site hosts a virtual museum exhibit that explains what Manzanar was like before, during, and after Japanese Americans lived there.

A More Perfect Union: Japanese Americans and the U.S. Constitution
http://amhistory.si.edu/perfectunion/experience/index.html
This Web site explores what Japanese Americans experienced while living in internment camps.

INDEX

ABOUT THE AUTHOR

Rachel Bailey grew up in a small Kansas town near Kansas City. Bailey is a former gifted-education teacher. She now writes children's books and magazine articles, as well as educational curriculum for teachers.